Mini-Moments
with
Angels

Mini-Moments
with
Angels

by Robert Strand

New Leaf Press

First printing: September 1997
Fifth printing: March 2008

ISBN-13: 978-0-89221-359-7
ISBN-10: 0-89221-359-0
Library of Congress Catalog No. 97-068954

Printed in the United States of America

Please visit our website for other great titles:
www.newleafpress.net

For information regarding author interviews, please contact the publicity department at (870) 438-5288.

Presented to:

_____

Presented by:

_____

Date:

_____

A Little Bit about Angels

Practically everybody knows something about angels . . . at least on some level. And it seems as if everybody is talking about angels today. You'll find boutiques dedicated to this subject, poetry exalts them, songs are created about them, and lots and lots of books are devoted to angels. Why? I think there is a deep, underlying need for all of us to have a glimpse into the spirit world about us. We are curious and hungry to learn more about this other world.

Let me point out a couple of things as we start: Never are we to worship angels. The Bible is explicitly clear that only God is to be worshiped. And the other thing is that we are not to pray to angels. It's okay to ask God for help, but not angels. Now . . . God may send an angel to answer your prayer. Let's explore this subject on these next few pages, but always keeping a healthy balance in regard to angels and this topic. ENJOY!

The angels are near to us, to those creatures
by God's command they are to preserve.

(Martin Luther)

Then I looked and heard the voice of many angels,
numbering thousands upon thousands, and ten thousand
times ten thousand. They encircled the throne
(Rev. 5:11).

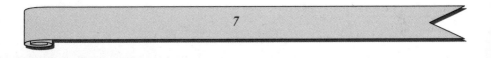

Just what do angels do and how do they work? It's a mystery . . . but there are enough stories and human encounters to give us a small clue. Are they always there in an emergency? Do they prevent it from happening or do they miraculously intervene?

Elisabeth Elliot has written a number of books, and one of particular interest is entitled *A Slow and Certain Light*. In it, she relates an experience her father had in regard to the possibility of angelic helpers. Here's her story:

"My father, when he was a small boy, was climbing on an upper story of a house that was being built. He walked to the end of a board that was not nailed at the other end, and it slowly began to tip. He knew that he was doomed, but inexplicably the board began to tip the other way, as though a hand had pushed it down again. He always wondered if it was an angel's hand."

Millions of spiritual creatures
walk the earth unseen, both when we sleep
and when we awake.
(John Milton)

See that you do not look down on one of these

little ones. For I tell you that their angels in

heaven always see the face of my Father in heaven

(Matt. 18:10).

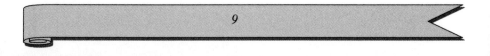

Billy Graham on Angels

The book that Billy Graham wrote, *Angels*, a Doubleday publication, was released so that sales began in October of 1975. By the following January, sales had reached the one million mark! It is believed to be the first time that a best seller has hit the one-million mark within such a short period of time . . . only four months!

Billy Graham says, "As an evangelist, I have often felt too far spent to minister from the pulpit to men and women who have filled stadiums to hear a message from the Lord. Yet again and again my weakness has vanished, and my strength has been renewed. I have been filled with God's power, not only in my soul but physically. On many occasions, God has become especially real, and has sent His unseen angelic visitors to touch my body to let me be His messenger for heaven, speaking as a dying man to dying men."

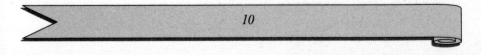

The helmed Cherubim, And sworded
Seraphim, Are seen in glittering ranks
with wings display'd.

(John Milton)

Are not all angels ministering spirits sent to serve

those who will inherit salvation?

(Heb. 1:14).

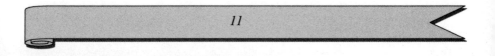

An angel is a spiritual creature created by God
without a body
for the service of Christendom
and of the Church.

Martin Luther (1483–1546)

Do You Have a Guardian Angel?

Basil the Great, way back in A.D. 379, said that every one of the faithful has a guardian angel, which was assigned at birth. What do they do? How about guarding?

Following a previous book I wrote about angels, I received a number of calls and notes from people sharing with me their angel story. Here's one:

"When I was a little girl, some of the neighbor kids and I, aged about five, six, and seven, were playing on a car, a coupe, with a long sloping trunk. We climbed up on the roof and slid down. As I slid down, I became impaled on a bumper guard. When I screamed, and the blood began to flow, all the kids became frightened and ran away, leaving me trapped and helpless to remove myself. A man dressed in gray appeared suddenly, who gently lifted me off the bumper guard and the pain disappeared as he carried me inside to my mother. Then, he disappeared. My mother attempted to follow him outside to express her thanks, but he was gone. Oh, yes, I was completely healed."

At birth, every person is given a
guardian angel who continually lights,
guards, rules, and guides.
(St. Thomas Aquinas)

But when we cried out to the Lord, He heard our cry and

sent an angel and brought us out of Egypt

(Num. 20:16).

Thinking Back

When Fred arrived at the Pearly Gates he didn't have to wait for his interview. Quickly he found himself standing before an impressive angelic being with a clipboard, who started his entry data. The angel said, "Fred, it would help if you could share with me an experience of a totally, purely unselfish deed from your life on earth."

Fred thought for a moment and replied, "Oh, yes. . . . One day I was walking along and I came upon a little old lady who was being robbed and beaten by a huge motorcycle gang type of fellow. Well, I kicked over his cycle . . . to distract him. Then I kicked him real hard in the shins and told the lady to run. Then I hauled off and gave the guy a great shot with my right."

The angel, impressed, said, "That's quite a story. Tell me, just when did this happen?"

Fred looked at his watch and said, "Oh, about two or three minutes ago."

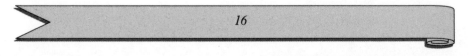

In these days you must go to
heaven to find an angel.
(Polish proverb)

When the angel of the Lord appeared to Gideon, he said,

"The Lord is with you, mighty warrior"

(Judg. 6:12).

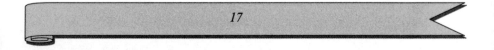

Angels are bright still,
though the brightest fell.

William Shakespeare (1564–1616)

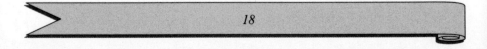

Perspective

The angels from their thrones on high
Look down on us with wondering eye,
That where we are but passing guests
We build such strong and solid nests,
And where we hope to dwell for aye
We scarce take heed a stone to lay.
(Author is unknown)

What is heaven like? Someone has said it like this: You land at the airport and there is God waiting to greet you. If you are a traveling person, you are also familiar with the sinking feeling that comes when you try to show people videos of the places you've been. You ask, "Who would like to see my videos?" And there is usually silence. All travelers have experienced that problem with friends and family.

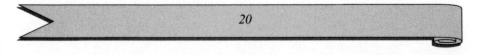

But with heaven, it goes this way: Not only is God at the airport saying "Welcome home! How was your trip?" God also says, "I would love to see your videos!"

Lutherans believe you cannot get into heaven
unless you bring a covered dish.
(Garrison Keilor)

Then I saw another mighty angel coming down from heaven.
He was robed in a cloud, with a rainbow above his head; his
face was like the sun, and his legs were like fiery pillars
(Rev. 10:1).

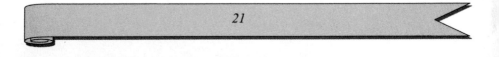

Have You Ever Seen an Angel?

Have you ever seen an angel? John G. Paton believes he has. While he was a missionary in the New Hebrides Islands, hostile natives surrounded his mission headquarters one night, intent on burning the Patons out and killing them. Paton and his wife prayed, terror stricken, all that night. At dawn, they were amazed to see the attackers just turn and leave.

A year later, the chief of that very tribe was converted to Christianity. Paton then asked him what had kept him and his men from burning down the house and killing them that night. The chief asked Paton a return question: "Who were all those men you had with you there?" Paton told him that there was just him and his wife, but the chief insisted they had seen hundreds of men standing guard . . . big men in shining garments with drawn swords.

Have you ever seen an angel?

What's impossible to all humanity
may be possible to the metaphysics and
physiology of angels.
(Joseph Glanvill)

The angel of the Lord encamps around those

who fear him, and he delivers them

(Ps. 34:7).

Praise ye the LORD: for it is good
to sing praises unto our God; for it
is pleasant; and praise is comely

(Ps. 147:2).

Back to Life

A 70-year-old lady was the only one who had knowledge of the daily operations of her family as well as the operations of their house church. She alone knew where the Bibles were, who the messengers were, and who could be trusted. She died suddenly of a heart attack.

The family was lost. She had not been able to pass on her important information. They began to pray: "Lord, restore our mother back to life." After being dead two days, she came back to life and scolded her family for calling her back. She didn't want to come back. They reasoned with her, and in two days, after she had helped them with the much-needed information, they would pray for her to go back to heaven.

After two days, the family and friends began to sing hymns and pray that the Lord would take her back. The mother's final words were: "They're coming. Two angels are coming." This incident caused the entire village to repent.

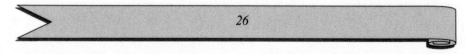

God employs them as messengers

to manifest himself to men.

(Calvin)

The harvest is the end of the age,

and the harvesters are angels

(Matt. 13:39).

A Soviet Witness to Angels

Perhaps you will remember this story from out of the past. It caused quite a sensation: Six Soviet cosmonauts said they witnessed the most awe-inspiring spectacle ever encountered in space . . . a band of glowing angels with wings as big as jumbo jets. According to *Weekly World News*, cosmonauts Vladimir Solovev, Oleg Atkov, and Leonid Kizim said they first saw the celestial beings during their 155th day aboard the orbiting "Salyat 7" space station. "What we saw," they said, "were seven giant figures in the form of humans, but with wings and mist-like halos, as in the classic depiction of angels. Their faces were round with cherubic smiles."

Twelve days later the figures returned and were seen by three other Soviet scientists, including woman cosmonaut Svetlann Savitskaya. "They were smiling," she said, "as though they shared in a glorious secret."

Look at it from their viewpoint . . . at least
they had proof of life in the hereafter.

(From the editor of *Parade* magazine,
as the bottom line when they printed this story)

Praise the Lord, you his angels,

you mighty ones who do his bidding,

who obey his word

(Ps. 103:20).

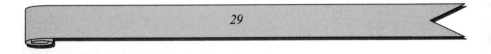

What Does an Angel Sound Like?

What does an angel sound like? What does an angel say? Upon doing some research on the times that angels spoke, I have discovered that an angel's voice sounds remarkably like one saying "Hurry up!"

We tend to think that angels speak in a beautiful, well-modulated tone. But the words "Get up!" are rarely beautiful, especially at 5:30 A.M. Yet, as you study the Bible, you will discover that angels are constantly saying, "Hurry up!" An angel appears in a jail cell and tells Peter, "Get up, quickly!" An angel prods Gideon with, "Rise up and get going!" An angel says to Elijah, "Get up and eat!" An angel appears to Joseph in a dream when Herod is killing all the infants and says, "Get going, quickly!" An angel makes an appearance to Philip and says, "Get up and get going!" Really . . . angels are monotonous talkers! They say the same thing: "Get up, get going, hurry!" Maybe a message for all of us for all time!

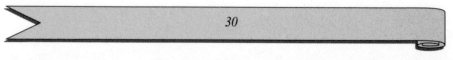

It is only with the heart that one can see
rightly; what is essential is invisible to the eye.
(Antoine DeSaint-Exupery)

Suddenly an angel of the Lord appeared

and a light shone in the cell. He struck Peter

on the side and woke him up. "Quick, get up!" he said,

and the chains fell off Peter's wrists

(Acts 12:7).

Angels guard you when you
walk with me.
What better way could you choose?

(Frances J. Roberts)

The Present Inhabitants of Heaven

Of all the supernatural beings mentioned in the Bible, it is the angels who are constantly pictured as being identified with heaven. When the angel of God appeared to Hagar while she was in the wilderness, the account says that the voice was "heard out of heaven." When the angels appeared to Jacob as he was running away, he saw a ladder reaching into heaven on which the angels of God were ascending and descending.

Often the angels are identified as "the heavenly ones" or the "heavenly host." When the angelic choir had finished their song to the shepherds on the hillside, we can read that these "angels went away from them into heaven." Then there was an "angel from heaven" who rolled away the stone at the tomb of Jesus Christ. Jesus often spoke of the "angels in heaven."

One more reason that I also want to be an inhabitant of heaven! How about you?

Think of him still as the same, I say,
He is not dead; he is just . . . away.
(James Whitcomb Riley)

No eye has seen, no ear has heard, no mind has conceived

what God has prepared for those who love him

(2 Cor. 2:9).

Open Your Eyes!

It was a very difficult situation. The king of Syria had sent a huge army, complete with horses and chariots, to surround the city. When the inhabitants got up the next morning they discovered the enemy army had circled them during the night. It was a hopeless situation! Surrounded, with all avenues of escape cut off. Not pretty. All could see for themselves . . . troops, horses, chariots, armor everywhere.

One frightened man went to his leader and in desperation asked, "What are we going to do now? There is no way out. We're goners!"

The first reply was, "Don't be afraid." Oh . . . sure. The answer continues, "Don't be afraid because our army is larger than theirs."

"Oh . . . but I can't see them."

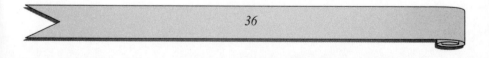

Then Elisha prayed, "Open his eyes and let him see!" And as his eyes were opened, he could see horses and chariots of fire everywhere upon the mountains! (Read the complete story from the biblical account in 2 Kings 6.)

This is what you are to hold fast to yourself . . . the sympathy and companionship of the unseen worlds.
(Phillips Brooks)

"Don't be afraid," the prophet answered. "Those who are with us are more than those who are with them"
(2 Kings 6:16).

Angels see only the light,

and devils only the darkness.

Jacob Bohme (1575–1624)

God's Special Messenger

This was related by a pastor who had gone to Mexico on a preaching mission:

While we were returning, our van developed mechanical problems. After jacking up the van, the pastor crawled under to check out the problem. The jack collapsed. He suddenly felt the crushing force against his chest. His companions quickly grabbed the bumper to lift the van. They weren't able to lift it. He cried out: "Jesus! Jesus!" Within seconds a youthful-looking Mexican came running to them. He was thin and small. His face was smiling. As he reached the van, he grabbed the bumper and lifted — it came up like a feather.

As he was freed, the pastor said he felt his chest expand and the broken bones mend. The visitor then lowered the van, waved to them, and ran in the direction from which he had come until he disappeared on the horizon.

It is for us to realize that God still sends His special messengers to protect His people.

Do not forget to entertain strangers, for by doing some

people have entertained angels without knowing it

(Heb. 13:2).

An Angel Brings Healing

Anthony had been desperately sick. His battle with kidney disease had landed him in the intensive care unit following a last-ditch surgical procedure. His life was hanging by a thread. He had no assurance of healing by his doctors. The family was called to be nearby. At times, Anthony wondered if he would survive another day.

He and his family had been praying . . . then, one early evening, when all hope had been dashed, a brilliant light, which he later described as "full of warmth and glory" filled his room in the ICU. Soon he became conscious of a tall, majestic angelic being standing by his bed, radiating a source of healing. The angel smiled and said, "Anthony, you will be all right." And then it was gone. Anthony said, "I felt like I was covered with a featherweight blanket of healing energy." Today he is well, completely whole!

Every breath of air and ray of light and heat,
every beautiful prospect, is, as it were, the
skirts of their garments, the waving of the
robes of those whose faces see God.
(John Henry Newman)

But the angel said to them, "Do not be afraid.

I bring you good news of great joy"

(Luke 2:10).

The angel of God said to me in the dream,

"Jacob." I answered, "Here I am"

(Gen. 31:11).

Disappearing Angels

Some angel stories keep recurring with the same kind of themes. These sound alike and you may have heard of one or more of these yourself. They go somewhat like this:

Two couples were vacationing together last summer in the West. They saw a woman standing by the road looking like she might be needing help. She had an unusually peaceful appearance, almost authoritative. They began to talk about the current events and phenomena of nature. One of them observes, "It seems like things are heading up for the soon return of the Lord."

The woman hitchhiker replies, "That will be sooner than you think!" And then . . . she is gone! The four friends are shocked, they stop and look around, no trace. So they stop in the next town to report at the police station only to hear the desk sergeant say, "You're the fifth to report this incident in the last 24-hour period."

Angels, as 'tis but seldom they appear
so neither do they make long stay;
they do but visit and away.
(John Norris)

See, I am sending an angel ahead of you to guard you along

the way and to bring you to the place I have prepared. Pay

attention to him and listen to what he says

(Exod. 23:20–21).

I See Angels!

The illness had been prolonged and marked by intense pain and suffering; cancer was slowly eating away the body of Joan's mother. On this particular night, Joan was seated by the hospital bedside of her mom and they had been quietly remembering many of the happy events of life together. This had been one of those wonderful experiences.

Suddenly, her mother sat bolt upright in bed, and with an expression of joyfulness said, "I can see my mother and father!" She paused, waited, then excitedly said, "I can see Jesus!" There was another pause, and "He's motioning for me to come! And . . . oh, Joan . . . I see the most beautiful angels!"

With this beautiful look of radiance, which Joan had never seen on her mother's face before, her mother laid back on the pillow and quietly passed from this life. Joan said, "The room seemed to be bathed in peace."

We are like children, who stand in need of masters to enlighten us and direct us; and God has provided for this, by appointing His angels to be our teachers and guides.
(Saint Thomas Aquinas)

For he will command his angels concerning you to guard you

in all your ways; they will lift you up in their hands

(Ps. 91:11).

*The angels are the dispensers
and administrators of the divine
beneficence toward us; they
regard our safety, undertake
our defense, direct our ways,
and exercise a constant
solicitude that no evil befall us.*

John Calvin (1509–1564)

The Warning

During WW II, James was a crew member on a B-29 bomber. They were flying over a part of central Europe on their way to a target in Germany. As they were making their final approach to the assigned target area, he felt a strong hand on his shoulder and a voice commanded, "Get up and go to the back of the plane!"

Almost immediately after he had made his way to the back of the plane, they came under a limited anti-aircraft attack. James waited a bit longer and sensed it would be safe to return to his seat in the front of the plane. When he returned, he immediately noticed that three shells had blown a hole in the ceiling of the plane, having entered from the bottom and penetrated his seat!

To this day, his confident explanation is that an angel had been sent to warn him!

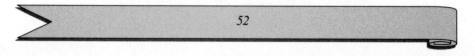

Every presence of an angel is a communication. Even when an angel crosses our path in silence, God has said to us, "I am here. I am present in your life."
(Tobias Palmer)

As she wept, she bent over to look into the tomb
and saw two angels in white, seated where Jesus' body
had been, one at the head and the other at the foot.
They asked her, "Woman, why are you crying?"
(John 20:11–12).

Who Are Angels?
What Are They Like?

Angels are created beings! The Bible indicates that they did not always exist. They report to God and are under His direct orders when on assignment. From the Bible we can say that angels are personal beings who represent God. The Book of the Revelation describes them as clothed with white robes and golden sashes. One angel in this book is described as being robed in a cloud with a rainbow over his head.

A French priest, Pere Lamy, describes angels like this: "Their garments are white, but with an unearthly whiteness. I cannot describe it, because it cannot be compared to earthly whiteness; it is much softer to the eye. These bright angels are enveloped in a light so different from ours that by comparison everything else seems dark. When you see a band of 50 you are lost in amazement. They seem clothed with golden plates, constantly moving, like so many suns."

Who does the best his circumstances
allows does well, acts nobly;
angels could do no more.
(Edward Young)

But even the archangel Michael, when he was

disputing with the devil about the body of Moses,

did not dare to bring a slanderous accusation

against him, but said, "The Lord rebuke you!"

(Jude 9).

The earth is to the sun what

man is to the angels.

Victor Hugo (1802–1885)

A Five-Year-Old Perspective

Five-year-old Betty was a little girl who had become frightened of thunderstorms which raged in her area of the upper Midwest during the summertime. So to comfort her, her mother had told her that the noise of a thunderstorm was not to be feared because it was only the angels making their beds.

One morning, after a particularly long and hard thunderstorm, marked by considerable thunder and lightning, the little girl said, "You know, Mommy, I didn't mind the noise when the angels made up their beds last night."

Her mother replied, "That was real good, honey."

Betty continued, "But I certainly did not like it when they couldn't make up their minds whether to turn the lights off or not."

It's easy to be an angel when nobody
ruffles your feathers.

*For the Lord himself will come down from heaven, with a
loud command, with the voice of the archangel and with the
trumpet call of God, and the dead in Christ will rise first*
(1 Thess. 4:16).

Angels on Assignment

It was a tragic night in an inland Chinese city. The bandits had come and dangers surrounded the mission compound which sheltered hundreds of woman and children. On the previous night, the missionary, Miss Monsen, had been put to bed with an attack of malaria.

She had prayed, "Lord, I have been teaching these people all these years that Your promises are true and if they fail now, my mouth shall be forever closed and I must go home."

All the next night she was up among the frightened refugees, encouraging them to trust in God and pray for deliverance. The raids continued all around them, but the compound was untouched by the violence.

In the morning, people from three neighboring families asked, "Who were those four people, three sitting and one standing, quietly watching from the top of your house all night long?"[1]

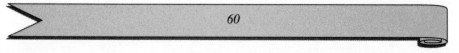

Weak men must fall,
for heaven still guards the right.
(Shakespeare, *Richard II*)

Last night an angel of the God whose I am and whom I

serve stood beside me and said "Do not be afraid"

(Acts 27:23–24).

The Lord is my strength and my song;

he has become my salvation.

He is my God, and I will praise him,

my father's God, and I will exalt him

(Exod. 15:2).

The Quick Trip

While serving in the Confederate Army, Henry M. Stanley was taken prisoner at the Battle of Shiloh and confined at Fort Douglas. In his autobiography he relates how, as he was one day playing cards, he felt a slight blow in the back of his neck and in a moment was by the bedside of his aunt in the farmhouse in Wales where he had lived for a year or more. His aunt lay dying and was asking his forgiveness for having turned him out into the world. He was about to take her hand when he "came to" and asked his card-playing buddies what had happened.

They wondered what he meant. The vision had been too quick. Later he received word telling him that, on the corresponding day and hour, his aunt had died and she left a message asking forgiveness of him.

Stanley goes on to say that he believes the intelligence of the swift vision was brought to him by a guardian angel and that every person has such a spirit.

To love for the sake of being loved is human,
but to love for the sake of loving is angelic.

(Alphonse-Marie-Louis de Prat de Lamartine)

So He became as much superior to the angels
as the name He has inherited is superior to theirs. For to
which of the angels did God ever say, "You are my Son;
today I have become your Father"?

(Heb. 1:4–5).

A Guardian Angel

There is an old tradition about the story of the apostle Peter being let out of prison by an angel who suddenly appeared. You can read the full story from the Book of Acts 12:1–19; you'll find it full of humor. The church was praying so earnestly and having faith in prayer that they didn't believe the deliverance when it happened. Read the story. Back to our original thought — just who was this guardian angel that made the timely appearance? We don't really know because the angel is identified as "an angel." But at this point, tradition comes to our rescue and tells us that this particular angel was Peter's mother!

Certainly, if such a task were to be assigned to those who have passed from this world into the world to come, surely a good mother would qualify for it better than most anyone else. At the least, we like to think that our mothers do surround us and follow us with their prayers, rejoicing over our successes and grieving over our hurts and wounds.

An angel is like you, Kate,
and you are like an angel.
(Shakespeare, *Henry V*)

Then the angel said to him,
"Put on your clothes and sandals."
And Peter did so.
"Wrap your cloak around you and follow me,"
the angel told him
(Acts 12:8).

The stars shine on brightly while Adam and
Eve pursue their way into the far wilderness.
There is a sound through the silence,
as of the falling tears of an angel.

Elizabeth Barrett Browning (1806–1861)

The Angels of Mons . . . Part I

According to a report in the London *Evening News*, Arthur Machen told how the tiny British expeditionary force, outnumbered three to one, was apparently saved by heavenly reinforcements. The angel, or angels, of Mons (and the accounts of their numbers have varied from one to a platoon), suddenly took up a position between them and the Germans. Understandably, the enemy fell back in confusion.

The battle took place on August 26, 1914, and when this story appeared in September, most of the survivors were still stationed in France. According to one other account, a British officer said that while his army was in retreat from Mons, a unit of German cavalry came charging after them. The British ran for a place from which to make a last stand, but the Germans got there first. Expecting almost certain death, the British troops turned and saw, to their astonishment, a troop of angels between them and the enemy. The German horses were terrified and stampeded in all directions.

The angels . . . regard our safety, undertake
our defense, direct our ways, and exercise a
constant solicitude that no evil befalls us.
(John Calvin)

God heard the boy crying, and the angel of God
called to Hagar from heaven and said to her,
"What is the matter, Hagar? Do not be afraid; God has
heard the boy crying as he lies there"
(Gen. 21:17).

A British army chaplain, the Rev. C.M. Chavasse, recorded that he had heard similar accounts to the miraculous Mons angelic deliverance from a brigadier general and two of his officers. A lieutenant colonel described how he, too, during this retreat, watched as his battalion was escorted for about 20 minutes by a host of phantom cavalry.

Then, from the German side came an account that their men refused to charge a certain point where the British line was broken because of the presence of a very large number of troops. According to Allied records of this battle, there was not a single British soldier in this immediate area.

What is noteworthy about these accounts is that not one of them is reported firsthand. In each case, officers wished to remain anonymous because it might hinder future promotions. Whatever the explanation . . . the British did achieve something of a miracle deliverance.

A guardian angel o'er his life presiding,
doubling his pleasures, and his cares dividing.
(Samuel Rogers)

He struggled with the angel and overcame him;
he wept and begged for his favor. He found him at Bethel
and talked with him there . . . the Lord God Almighty,
the Lord is His name of renown!
(Hos. 12:4–5).

When angels come,
the devils leave.

(Arabian proverb)

Unaccustomed Praise

This man, who never praised his wife, happened to be in attendance at his local Rotary service club when the speaker encouraged the men to compliment their wives more than they had been doing. It would improve home life, the speaker had said. He thought it would be a good idea, so he decided to call her an angel. "Mary," he said one morning, "you are an angel!" She was impressed and felt charmed and special all day long.

But a wife being a wife, she wanted to know more, so she ventured to ask why she had been so honored by him on that morning.

"Well," replied the wily one, "in the first place you are always flitting about; second, you are always up in the air about something; thirdly, you are always harping about something; and fourthly, by your own account you don't have a heavenly thing to wear."

This world has angels all too few,
and heaven is overflowing.
(S.T. Coleridge)

It was revealed to them that they were not
serving themselves but you, when they spoke of the
things that have now been told you by those who have
preached the gospel to you by the Holy Spirit sent from
heaven. Even angels long to look into these things
(1 Pet. 1:12).

Angelic Deliverance

Angie grew up in one of those charming small towns along the Mississippi delta. She was eight years old and one of her duties was to walk home from school every day with her little six-year-old brother. The best part of their daily walk on the tree-lined street was to pause in front of one of those beautiful southern large brick houses. The gardens were gorgeous, and surrounded by an ornate wrought-iron fence, painted white.

On this particular afternoon, as they paused to enjoy the mansion before them . . . she and her brother felt a hand on their shoulders, lifting them and gently placing them about 15 or 20 feet away. At that same instant . . . a car, out of control, speeding, jumped the curb and smashed into the iron fence . . . at the spot where they had been standing! When Angie and her little brother had recovered, they turned around to see who had picked them up . . . no one was to be seen!

Angels don't submit to litmus tests,
testify in court, or slide under
a microscope for examinations.
(Joan Wester Anderson)

Then the Lord spoke to the angel,

and he put his sword back into its sheath

(1 Chron. 21:27).

When Gideon realized that it was the angel of the LORD, he exclaimed, "Ah, Sovereign LORD! I have seen the angel of the LORD face to face!"
(Judg. 6:22).

A Fallen Angel

The American adventurer Jimmy Angel is credited with discovering the highest waterfall in the world. This he spotted from the air in 1935 while prospecting for gold in the Guiana Highlands of Venezuela. He was intrigued by the sight and determined to return.

Two years later he did return . . . flying a single-engine airplane which he crashed while attempting to make a landing on the plateau above the falls.

He survived the crash and lived to tell about it and the falls. This spectacular 3,212 foot waterfall was consequently named "Salto Angel" or the "Fallen Angel" after Jimmy.

But Angel was not the first outsider, non-Indian to have seen the spectacular, world's-highest cascade on the Churun River. This waterfall plunging down the side of Auyan Tepui ("Devil's Mountain"), had been reported by a Spanish explorer, Ernesto Sanches La Cruz, in 1910.

Therefore, with Angels and Archangels,
and with all the company of heaven,
we laud and magnify thy glorious Name;
evermore praising thee.
(Book of Common Prayer)

He will cover you with his feathers, and under
his wings you will find refuge; his faithfulness
will be your shield and rampart. You will not fear
the terror of night, nor the arrow that flies by day
(Ps. 91:4–5).

Why Study Angels?

This is a valid question . . . and is extremely important because so much of the Bible is devoted to angels. They are seen in historical narratives which reflect God's love and judgment.

"Angelology" leads us to appreciate the holiness of God. Angels do the will of God. Angels let us see what these divine intelligences provide in the way of resources. The study of angels increases faith in Almighty God's care and grace. Think of the immense awesomeness in God's sending beings of such high rank to minister to human beings. Angelology generates humility in the Christians who properly understand that angels are high beings who do many unnoticed services for God. People and angels have the same Heavenly Father! This study increases the Christian's feelings of dignity. When we face trials, tests, temptations, and difficulties, it is a comfort to realize that we have God, plus the elect angels of heaven!

Many people who do not believe in the inerrancy of the Scriptures have a low view of angelology, and they ascribe little importance to the teaching of angels who are seen only as a product of Persian mythology.
(Thomas F. Harrison)

There the angel of the Lord appeared to him in flames of fire from within a bush. Moses saw that though the bush was on fire it did not burn up
(Exod. 3:2).

I surely must be going now,

my strength sinks so fast.

What glory!

The angels are waiting for me!

(Thomas Bateman)

Snakebitten!

Jason was an active, outdoorsy, 12 year old, who lived with his family on the edge of a wooded, swampy area. They were the last farm on their road before you would have plunged off into the wilderness. Jason developed an avid interest in snakes. His favorite thing to do was take an old sock with him in which he could carry home another snake or two.

On this day he didn't notice the coiled water moccasin. He felt the hard hit on the back of his upper calf, then searing pain began running up his leg. He knew immediately what had happened. He walked a few steps, then dropped to the ground. The effects of the adult snake's venom was already starting to work! No one knew where he was! How could he get help? He cried out for help, but no one answered. Then he prayed! Almost immediately a man appeared, picked him up, and carried him to the farm house. Mom and Dad called 911, put him in their pickup, and rushed to the local hospital emergency room! With the injection of anti-venom, Jason survived. But without the help of the anonymous stranger, the doctor said he would have died!

Angels — they happen when you least expect them and need them the most.

With the coming of dawn, the angels urged Lot, saying, "Hurry! Take your wife and your two daughters who are here, or you will be swept away"

(Gen. 19:15).

The Emergency Call

Lou was a busy self-made entrepreneur who also made time in his hectic life to serve his small community as a volunteer fireman. The week had been full and busy — but as he drove home on Saturday afternoon, he had other things on his mind. It was time to kick back and relax in front of the TV, watching his beloved Nebraska Cornhuskers. Just before halftime, the phone rang . . . emergency fire call — he was needed immediately!

He grabbed his gear and ran out the door to his pickup in the driveway. He jumped in, started it, and was ready to back out. Then, suddenly, there was a presence standing by his open window. He did a double take and it spoke, "Don't back out. Look behind you first." Even though Lou was in a hurry, the urgency of the command led him to get out and walk behind the truck. There was a little four-year-old neighbor boy sitting on his trike, leaning against the bumper and watching the clouds go by!

How many angels are there? One . . . who
transforms our life . . . is plenty.
(Traditional)

Do you think I cannot call on my Father, and he will at

once put at my disposal more than twelve legions of angels?

(Matt. 26:53).

God often visits us, but most of the time
we are not at home.

(Polish proverb)

Housework by an Angel

Gladys Triplett barely had enough strength to answer the doorbell that morning in 1941 in Newberg, Oregon. Not recovered from the birth of their eighth child, she had spent a sleepless night, and although it was only 10:30 A.M. she was exhausted. She felt too weak to tackle the mountain of dirty dishes, unmade beds, meals, and the huge pile of laundry. Her husband was absent on a speaking engagement.

The plainly dressed woman at the door said, "The Father has sent me to minister to you, because of your distress and great need. You called with all your heart and you asked in faith."

Then lifting Gladys, the stranger laid her on the couch and said, "Your Heavenly Father heard your prayer. Sleep now, my child." When Gladys awoke three hours later, refreshed, the change in the house was amazing! Dishes were done, floors were clean, toys picked up, baby had been bathed and was sleeping, dining room table was set, food prepared, laundry done, and ironing finished! Who was she? No human could have done so much in only three hours![2]

Never did the messengers claim to be angels, but their sudden disappearance, and the fact that no one in the vicinity had known about them, lend credence to the belief that angelic ministry occurred. If not, where did the unusual help come from?
(Ralph W. Harris)

Praise him, all his angels, praise him, all his heavenly hosts
(Ps. 148:2).

The Large Army

The gospel story of Jesus Christ had been taken to a village deep in the interior of Brazil. Through the years, many of these villagers accepted Jesus as Lord and Savior. Over time, this made the people in the next village very angry because these Christians no longer would buy or trade with them in their idol-making. Eventually this led to the angry villagers vowing to come over the pass to kill them all.

The people in the Christianized village went to prayer about the threats. Days, then weeks went by and still no attack. Some months later the chief of the warring village came over to talk to the leader of the Christian village. The people asked why his village had not come over the pass to make war against them?

The chief said they had attempted to, but as they started up the pass, they were met by a large army with drawn swords on white horses blocking their way. Afraid, they turned and ran.

Not angles, but Angels!
(Latin: *Non angli, sed Angeli!*)
(Gregory the Great)

After he drove the man out, he placed on the east side

of the Garden of Eden cherubim and a flaming sword

flashing back and forth to guard the way

(Gen. 3:24).

After this I saw another angel coming down from heaven. He had great authority, and the earth was illuminated by his splendor

(Rev. 18:1).

How Do You Verify an Angel Story?

Has the question or thought occurred to you: How can these angel stories be verified? The Bible records many incidents concerning the ministry of angels and their supernatural help. And the authority of the Bible speaks for itself. It is beyond question.

But what if you have experienced an angel happening? Or if someone you know has told about an angel ministry? Or what about these we have been reading? How do we verify these? To be candid, we must depend solely upon the sources, the people involved. Many of these incidents cannot be documented in any other way.

And perhaps this is the very reason why you may have doubts. We must depend on the honesty and integrity of the people sharing these experiences. Maybe this is the reason why some people may have had an angel happening but are reluctant to share it. So, if we believe in the supernatural, we must also have faith in the human messengers.

Around our pillows golden ladders rise,
and up and down the skies,
with winged sandals shod,
the angels come, and go,
the Messengers of God!
(R.H. Stoddard)

The angel of the Lord said to Elijah the Tishbite,
"Go up and meet the messengers of the king of Samaria and
ask them, 'Is it because there is no God in Israel that you are
going off to consult Baal-Zebub, the god of Ekron?' "
(2 Kings 1:3).

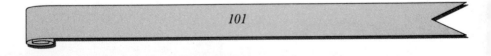

What Do Angels Look Like?

The well-known artist Rockwell Kent had been painting for some time in order to prepare his art for a showing. The day came to open the exhibit to the public. There was quite a crowd of people who had gathered to see his works, especially his paintings of angels. The artist was making his way through the crowd, answering questions, meeting people, explaining some of his works, when he came on a lady who had been staring intently at one of his celebrated angel paintings. Spotting the artist coming toward her, she approached him, pointed to the painting, and exclaimed, "No angel ever looked like that!"

To which the artist, without emotion asked, "Have you ever seen an angel, Madam?"

Now, that is quite the question. Have you ever seen an angel? It's quite possible that you have and not even been aware of the angelic presence. From the Bible, they assumed all kinds of appearances . . . from strangers, to heavenly beings, to armed warriors, to chariot drivers, to simply being a visitor.

Like the patriarch's angel,
hold it fast till it gives its blessing.
(Whittier)

Then the man said, "Let me go, for it is daybreak." But

Jacob replied, "I will not let you go unless you bless me"

(Gen. 32:26).

Beyond this vale of tears
There is a life above
Unmeasured by the flight of years
And all that life is love.

(James Montgomery)

Now the Day Is Over

Now the day is over, night is drawing nigh,
Shadows of the evening steal across the sky.

Jesus give the weary, calm and sweet repose,
With thy tenderest blessing, may our eyelids close.

Grant to little children visions bright of thee,
Guard the sailors tossing on the deep blue sea.

Through the long night-watches, may thy angels spread
Their white wings above me, watching round my bed.

When the morning wakens, then may I arise
Pure and fresh and sinless in thy holy eyes.

(Sabine Baring-Gould)

And so thy path shall be a track of light, like
angels' footsteps passing through the night.
(Words from a church in Upwaltham, England)

But the angel of the Lord called out to him from
heaven, "Abraham! Abraham!" "Here I am," he replied.
"Do not lay a hand on the boy," he said. "Do not do
anything to him. Now I know that you fear God, because
you have not withheld from me your son"
(Gen. 22:11–12).

Footprints in the Snow

Dustin, my California-bred guide dog, was having trouble outside our Long Island apartment. This was his first snowstorm and he was confused. I'm blind, and I wasn't doing so well, either. No one was out, so there were no sounds to steer me. Contrary to what many people think, guide dogs do not find the way for a blind person, the blind person directs the dog.

After a harrowing 45 minutes, Dustin and I made it back. Guide dogs must be walked regularly. "Next time, why don't you ask God to go with you?" a friend offered. So I did.

Snow stung our faces and it was difficult to make a path. Dustin whined a little. "Okay, boy," I said to him, "the Lord is with us." And then I gave him a command that a blind person gives only when another person is leading the way: "Dustin, follow!" Dustin perked up and took off. We made it and then headed back to our building. A young woman offered to walk us to our door. "We'll just follow your footprints," she said. "Yours and the dog's, and that other person's."[3]

Oh yes, there was Someone with us.
There always is!
(Sandy Seltzer)

The Angel who has delivered me from all harm . . .
may he bless these boys. May they be called by my
name and the names of my fathers Abraham and Isaac,
and may they increase greatly upon the earth
(Gen. 48:16).

By heaven we understand a state of happiness
infinite in degree and endless in duration.

Benjamin Franklin (1706–1790)

What Policeman?

The Curt Steen family was traveling on I-35 through Iowa in a snowstorm. As they traveled, the storm kept getting more fierce in intensity. Travel was slow and harrowing, but they decided to keep on going, thinking they might drive out of it near the Missouri border. But of real concern to them at the moment was the gas gauge in their Lincoln. It was on empty! The storm had closed down everything. The family prayed for help.

It was critical that they find fuel. At the next small town exit they turned off and went in search of help. A town police officer stopped and told them to follow him to a station to which he had a key and could get them some gas. They followed and fueled. He refused their offer to pay and they drove off. They had not gone far when one of the girls said, "We didn't thank the man." So they turned around and drove back to the station, only to find it an abandoned station, obviously not in service for years. They drove around looking for the officer and stopped a person to inquire about the town cop only to be told they did not have a town cop!

We may not experience the supernatural deliverance of an angel, but God promises us supernatural strength of spirit. Our faith and trust are made stronger and our character is strengthened when we pass through storms without the help of angels.
(Hope MacDonald)

At that time men will see the Son of Man coming in clouds with great power and glory. And He will send His angels and gather His elect from the four winds, from the ends of the earth to the ends of the heavens (Mark 13:26-27).

Protection in Israel

Evangelist Frankie Walker relates the following: In August of 1990 my next assignment was in Israel. The Gulf War was threatening to go full-scale and Saddam Hussein was a great threat at this time. This one experience was to do with Jerusalem.

I had not been able to go to the Upper Room and I was determined to make a visit there. On Sunday after church, I headed for the Damascus Gate, and just before the street I was to turn down to go there, I had one of the strongest impressions not to go and instead go to the YMCA for tea. I ordered my tea and sat there for a short time when some people from Europe came and sat at the table next to mine. In a loud and clear voice I overheard one man say, "I'm glad we were not inside the Damascus Gate when the riots broke out." Then another added, "They had all those homemade bombs and the knives and rocks were flying and they destroyed the police booth and locked out the police that came to reinforce the soldiers who were inside."

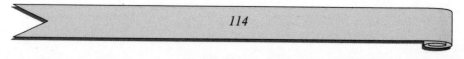

Praise welled up inside of me for such a directive which kept me safe that day.[4]

Half of Americans . . . and three-fourths of
teenagers believe in angels.
(1990 Gallup poll)

The Son of Man will send out his angels,
and they will weed out of his kingdom everything
that causes sin and all who do evil
(Matt. 13:41).

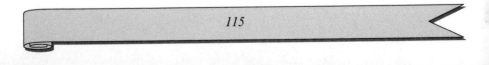

The angel went to her and said,
"Greetings, you who are highly favored!
The Lord is with you"

(Luke 1:28).

The Message

After the Sabbath, as the first light of the new week dawned, Mary Magdalene and the other Mary came to keep vigil at the tomb. Suddenly the earth reeled and rocked under their feet as God's angel came down from heaven and came right up to where they were standing. He rolled back the stone and then sat on it. Shafts of lightning blazed from him. His garments shimmered snow-white. The guards at the tomb were scared to death. They were so frightened they couldn't move.

The angel spoke to the women: "There is nothing to fear here. I know you're looking for Jesus, the one they nailed to the cross. He is not here. He was raised, just as He said. Come and look at the place where He was placed.

"Now, get on your way quickly and tell His disciples, 'He is risen from the dead. He is going on ahead of you to Galilee. You will see Him there.' That's the message!" (Matt. 28:1–7).[5]

I believe in angels because I have sensed their presence in my life on special occasions.
(Billy Graham)

Jesus did many other miraculous signs in the presence of his disciples, which are not recorded in this book. But these are written that you may believe that Jesus is the Christ, the Son of God, and that by believing you may have life in his name
(John 20:30–31).

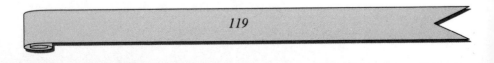

A Final Thought . . . or Two

How do people living in our culture deal with anything called "supernatural"? How do you? Are we comfortable with the spirit world? How do you explain such phenomena as we have been reading about?

Why should we have to explain such happenings? Is it so hard to believe that a kind, caring, loving Heavenly Father would willingly send angels to do some of His work for people who live on this earth? Why not? We have discovered that angels can bring good news, provide when there are needs, protect when someone may be in danger, guide those who may be lost, give practical help, bring healing, or simply stand by. They are lifters and helpers!

Now, when we stop to think about it, we could also do some of those same things for each other! Few of us may actually have a heavenly encounter during our lifetime, but . . . we can all learn how to respond to someone's need! And think of how much better this place would be because of it!

There is one trouble with full-time angels;
they are completely unpredictable and you
cannot send out for one. That is why
part-time angels are so important.
Part-time angels like you and me.
(Lee Ballard)

*The angel said to me, "These words are
trustworthy and true. The Lord, the God of the
spirits of the prophets, sent His angel to show His
servants the things that must soon take place"*
(Rev. 22:6).

Endnotes

1 Carl Lawrence, *The Church in China* (Minneapolis, MN: Bethany House, 1985), p. 76–77, adapted.

2 Ralph W. Harris, *Acts Today* (Springfield, MO: Gospel Publishing House, 1995), p. 138, adapted and condensed.

3 Sandy Seltzer, *Footprints in the Snow*, First Dimensions for Living edition (Carmel, NY: Guideposts Associates, Inc., 1992), condensed.

4 Frankie Walker, who told this to the author.

5 Eugene H. Peterson, *The Message* (Colorado Springs, CO: Navpress, Alive Communications, 1993).

If you enjoyed this book we also have available:

Mini-Moments for Christmas
Mini-Moments for Fathers
Mini-Moments for Graduates
Mini-Moments for Leaders
Mini-Moments for Mothers

At Christian bookstores nationwide